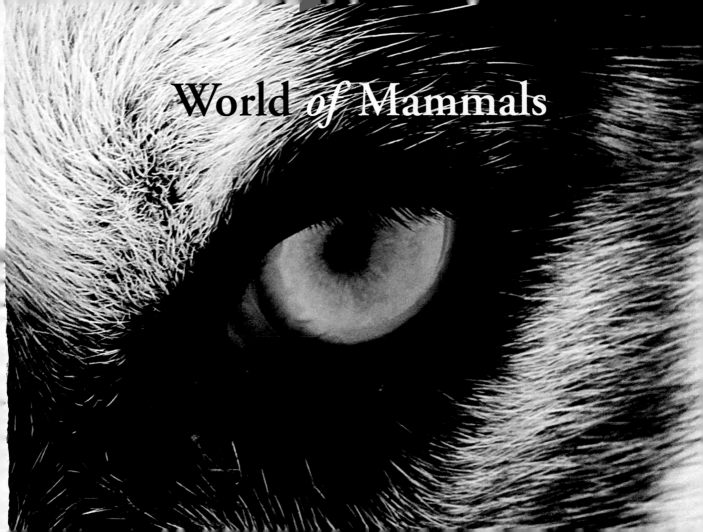

World *of* Mammals

World *of*

Mammals

Introducing the World of Mammals

The planet's mammal fauna is certainly diverse, and it encompasses everything from ocean-dwelling giants such as the Blue Whale, through to egg-laying echidnas, winged animals such as bats, mole-rats which spend their entire lives underground, and tiny shrews. As well as taking many different forms, the mammals include species with highly varied lifestyles, from solitary creatures such as leopards, which only generally come together for breeding, through to the likes of reindeer and wildebeest which form herds millions strong.

Mammals can also be found in just about every habitat available – enduring extremes of heat, cold and altitude – and on every continent. What draws the mammals together and gives them common ground is that they have hair or fur to a greater or lesser extent, and the fact that all nourish their young with milk.

The exact number of mammal species extant on Earth varies according to which authority you consult but, for example, according to the ASM Mammal Diversity Database (mammaldiversity.org) it is currently considered to be somewhere in the region of 6,500 species. For the purposes of classification, this book draws on that listing, while the taxonomic order and nomenclature adheres broadly to the third edition of Don E. Wilson and DeeAnn M. Reeder's *Mammal Species of the World. A Taxonomic and Geographic Reference* (Johns Hopkins University Press).

At present some of these mammals are flourishing while others are clinging on to existence by a thread. Of course, many species are threatened with extinction due to human induced habitat destruction and climate change that are fuelled by the metaphorical elephant in the room that is unchecked exponential human population growth, which no politician or environmental activist seems willing to address at present! Hopefully some day soon…

From the common to the rare, *World of Mammals* distils this extraordinary diversity down into about 250 images illustrating nearly 250 species and as wide a variety of the different mammal forms as possible from 25 orders and nearly 120 families. We hope that you enjoy this book and its amazing images, and that it contributes towards inspiring further interest in mammals and their conservation worldwide.

Short-beaked Echidna *Tachyglossus aculeatus*
AUSTRALIA AND NEW GUINEA

Platypus *Ornithorhynchus anatinus*
AUSTRALIA

Bare-tailed Woolly Opossum *Caluromys philander*
NORTHERN SOUTH AMERICA

Brazilian Gracile Opossum *Gracilinanus microtarsus*
SOUTH-EAST BRAZIL

CARNIVOROUS MARSUPIALS
– DASYUROMORPHIA

Numbat *Myrmecobius fasciatus*
WESTERN AUSTRALIA

Eastern Quoll *Dasyurus viverrinus*
TASMANIA (EXTINCT MAINLAND AUSTRALIA)

Tasmanian Devil *Sarcophilus harrisii*
TASMANIA

Yellow-footed Antechinus *Antechinus flavipes*
AUSTRALIA

Fat-tailed Dunnart *Sminthopsis crassicaudata*

Greater Bilby *Macrotis lagotis*
AUSTRALIA

Southern Brown Bandicoot   *Isoodon obesulus*
AUSTRALIA

Koala *Phascolarctos cinereus*
AUSTRALIA

Common Wombat *Vombatus ursinus*
AUSTRALIA

Western Pygmy Possum *Cercartetus concinnus*

Sulawesi Bear Cuscus *Ailurops ursinus*

SULAWESI

Common Brushtail Possum *Trichosurus vulpecula*
AUSTRALIA

Common Ringtail Possum *Pseudocheirus peregrinus*
AUSTRALIA

Sugar Glider *Petaurus breviceps*
AUSTRALIA

Honey Possum   *Tarsipes rostratus*
WESTERN AUSTRALIA

Feather-tailed Glider *Acrobates pygmaeus*
AUSTRALIA

Musky Rat-kangaroo *Hypsiprymnodon moschatus*
AUSTRALIA

Eastern Bettong *Bettongia gaimardi*

Long-nosed Potoroo *Potorous tridactylus*
AUSTRALIA

Goodfellow's Tree-kangaroo *Dendrolagus goodfellowi*
PAPUA NEW GUINEA

Eastern Grey Kangaroo *Macropus giganteus*
AUSTRALIA

Red-necked Wallaby *Macropus rufogriseus*
AUSTRALIA

Yellow-footed Rock Wallaby *Petrogale xanthopus*
AUSTRALIA

Red-legged Pademelon *Thylogale stigmatica*
AUSTRALIA

TENRECS AND ALLIES – AFROSORICIDA

Lesser Hedgehog Tenrec *Echinops telfairi*
MADAGASCAR

Lowland Streaked Tenrec *Hemicentetes semispinosus*
MADAGASCAR

ELEPHANT SHREWS – MACROSCELIDEA

Bushveld Elephant Shrew   *Elephantulus intufi*

Eastern Rock Elephant Shrew *Elephantulus myurus*
SOUTHERN AFRICA

Aardvark *Orycteropus afer*
SUB-SAHARAN AFRICA

Rock Hyrax *Procavia capensis*

AFRICA

Asian Elephant   *Elephas maximus*
SOUTH ASIA

African Elephant *Elephas africana*
SUB-SAHARAN AFRICA

Dugong *Dugong dugon*
COASTS OF INDIAN AND WEST PACIFIC OCEANS

West Indian Manatee *Trichechus manatus*
COASTS AND RIVERS OF CARIBBEAN AND GULF OF MEXICO

Nine-banded Armadillo *Dasypus novemcinctus*

Brown-throated Sloth *Bradypus variegatus*

CENTRAL AND SOUTH AMERICA

Hoffmann's Two-toed Sloth *Choloepus hoffmanni*

Giant Anteater *Myrmecophaga tridactyla*
CENTRAL AND SOUTH AMERICA

Southern Tamandua   *Tamandua tetradactyla*
SOUTH AMERICA

Northern Treeshrew *Tupaia belangeri*
SOUTH AND SOUTH-EAST ASIA

Sunda Flying Lemur *Galeopterus variegatus*
SOUTH-EAST ASIA

Eastern Rufous Mouse Lemur *Microcebus rufus*

Alaotra Bamboo Lemur   *Hapalemur alaotrensis*

MADAGASCAR

Red Ruffed Lemur *Varecia rubra*

MADAGASCAR

White-footed Sportive Lemur *Lepilemur leucopus*
MADAGASCAR

Verreaux's Sifaka *Propithecus verreauxi*

Bengal Slow Loris *Nycticebus bengalensis*
SOUTH ASIA

Moholi Bushbaby *Galago moholi*
SOUTHERN AFRICA

Spectral Tarsier *Tarsius tarsier*

SULAWESI

Pygmy Marmoset *Callithrix pygmaea*
SOUTH AMERICA

White-headed Capuchin   *Cebus capucinus*
CENTRAL AND SOUTH AMERICA

Azara's Night Monkey *Aotus azarae*
SOUTH AMERICA

Lucifer Titi *Callicebus lucifer*
SOUTH AMERICA

Black Howler *Alouatta caraya*
SOUTH AMERICA

Vervet Monkey *Chlorocebus pygerythrus*
SUB-SAHARAN AFRICA

Black Crested Mangabey *Lophocebus aterrimus*
DEMOCRATIC REPUBLIC OF CONGO

Japanese Macaque *Macaca fuscata*
JAPAN

Chacma Baboon *Papio ursinus*
SOUTHERN AFRICA

Gelada   *Theropithecus gelada*
ETHIOPIA

Mantled Guereza *Colobus guereza*

AFRICA

Tufted Grey Langur *Semnopithecus priam*
INDIA AND SRI LANKA

Lar Gibbon *Hylobates lar*
SOUTH-EAST ASIA

Eastern Gorilla *Gorilla beringei*
EAST AFRICA

Human *Homo sapiens*
WORLDWIDE

Chimpanzee *Pan troglodytes*
EQUATORIAL AFRICA

Sumatran Orangutan *Pongo abelii*
SUMATRA

Indian Giant Squirrel *Ratufa indica*

Central American Dwarf Squirrel *Microsciurus alfari*
CENTRAL AMERICA

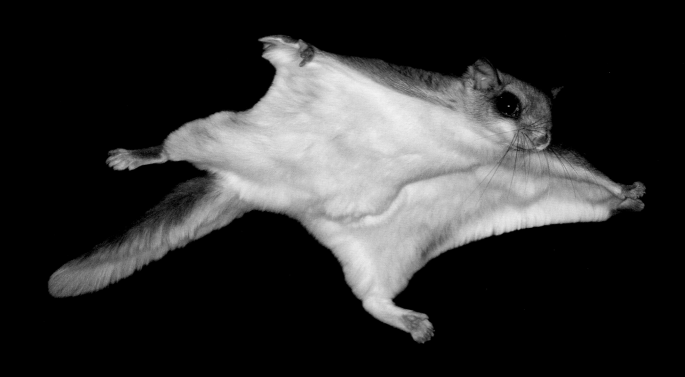

Southern Flying Squirrel   *Glaucomys volans*
NORTH AMERICA

Striped Ground Squirrel *Xerus erythropus*
SUB-SAHARAN AFRICA

Black-tailed Prairie Dog *Cynomys ludovicianus*
NORTH AMERICA

Eastern Chipmunk *Tamias striatus*

NORTH AMERICA

Hazel Dormouse *Muscardinus avellanarius*
EUROPE

American Beaver *Castor canadensis*
NORTH AMERICA

Merriam's Kangaroo Rat   *Dipodomys merriami*
NORTH AMERICA

Desert Pocket Mouse *Chaetodipus penicillatus*
NORTH AMERICA

Botta's Pocket Gopher *Thomomys bottae*
WESTERN NORTH AMERICA

Williams's Jerboa *Allactaga williamsi*
MIDDLE EAST

Woodland Jumping Mouse *Napaeozapus insignis*
NORTH AMERICA

Great Balkhan Calomyscus *Calomyscus mystax*
CENTRAL ASIA

Lesser Mole-Rat *Nanospalax leucodon*
EASTERN EUROPE

Ethiopian Mole-Rat *Tachyoryctes microcephalus*
ETHIOPIA

Stoliczka's Mountain Vole *Alticola stoliczkanus*

Northern Mole Vole *Ellobius talpinus*
RUSSIA

Norway Lemming *Lemmus lemmus*
NORTHERN EUROPE

Field Vole *Microtus agrestis*
EURASIA

Bank Vole *Myodes glareolus*
EURASIA

Common Muskrat *Ondatra zibethicus*

Striped Desert Hamster   *Phodopus sungorus*
CENTRAL ASIA

Bushy-tailed Woodrat *Neotoma cinerea*
NORTH AMERICA

North American Deermouse *Peromyscus maniculatus*

Arizona Cotton Rat *Sigmodon arizonae*
NORTH AMERICA

North-east African Spiny Mouse *Acomys cahirinus*
NORTH-EAST AFRICA

Indian Desert Jird *Meriones hurriane*
SOUTH ASIA

Lesser Egyptian Gerbil *Gerbillus gerbillus*
NORTH AFRICA AND MIDDLE EAST

Harvest Mouse *Micromys minutus*
EURASIA

House Mouse *Mus musculus*
WORLDWIDE

Brown Rat *Rattus norvegicus*
WORLDWIDE

South African Spring Hare *Pedetes capensis*
SOUTHERN AFRICA

Common Gundi *Ctenodactylus gundi*

NORTH AFRICA

Cape Mole-Rat *Georychus capensis*
SOUTH AFRICA

Naked Mole-Rat *Heterocephalus glaber*

Cape Porcupine *Hystrix africaeaustralis*
SOUTHERN AFRICA

Dassie Rat *Petromus typicus*
SOUTHERN AFRICA

North American Porcupine *Erethizon dorsatum*
NORTH AMERICA

Orange-spined Hairy Dwarf Porcupine *Sphiggurus villosus*
BRAZIL

Short-tailed Chinchilla *Chinchilla chinchilla*
SOUTH AMERICA

Southern Mountain Viscacha   *Lagidium vizcacha*
SOUTH AMERICA

Brazilian Guinea Pig *Cavia aperea*
SOUTH AMERICA

Capybara *Hydrochaeris hydrochaeris*
SOUTH AMERICA

Mexican Agouti *Dasyprocta mexicana*
MEXICO

Common Degu *Octodon degus*
CHILE

Amazon Bamboo Rat *Dactylomys dactylinus*
SOUTH AMERICA

Coypu *Myocastor coypus*
SOUTH AMERICA

Desmarest's Hutia *Capromys pilorides*

CUBA

PIKAS AND RABBITS – LAGOMORPHA

American Pika *Ochotona princeps*
NORTH AMERICA

Snowshoe Hare *Poecilolagus americanus*

NORTH AMERICA

Brown Hare *Lepus europaeus*
EURASIA

European Rabbit   *Oryctolagus cuniculus*
EURASIA, INTRODUCED WORLDWIDE

European Hedgehog *Erinaceus europaeus*
EUROPE

Desert Hedgehog *Paraechinus aethiopicus*
NORTH AFRICA AND MIDDLE EAST

Short-tailed Gymnure *Hylomys suillus*
SOUTH-EAST ASIA

Lesser White-toothed Shrew *Crocidura suaveolens*
EURASIA

Eurasian Water Shrew *Neomys fodiens*

EURASIA

Common Shrew *Sorex araneus*
EUROPE

Star-nosed Mole *Condylura cristata*
NORTH AMERICA

European Mole *Talpa europaea*
EURASIA

Peters's Lesser Epauletted Fruit Bat *Micropteropus pusillus*
SUB-SAHARAN AFRICA

Lyle's Flying Fox *Pteropus lylei*
SOUTH-EAST ASIA

Egyptian Rousette *Rousettus aegyptiacus*
AFRICA AND SOUTH-WEST ASIA

Mehely's Horseshoe Bat   *Rhinolophus mehelyi*
MEDITERRANEAN TO MIDDLE EAST

Persian Trident Bat *Triaenops persicus*
MIDDLE EAST AND EAST AFRICA

Lesser False Vampire Bat *Megaderma spasma*
SOUTH ASIA

Mauritian Tomb Bat *Taphozous mauritianus*
SUB-SAHARAN AFRICA

Egyptian Slit-faced Bat *Nycteris thebaica*
AFRICA AND MIDDLE EAST

Common Vampire Bat *Desmodus rotundus*
SOUTH AMERICA

Pallas's Long-tongued Bat *Glossophaga soricina*
CENTRAL AMERICA AND SOUTH AMERICA

Fringe-lipped Bat *Trachops cirrhosus*
SOUTH AMERICA, CENTRAL AMERICA AND CARIBBEAN

Brazilian Free-tailed Bat *Tadarida brasiliensis*
AMERICAS

Common Pipistrelle *Pipistrellus pipistrellus*
EURASIA

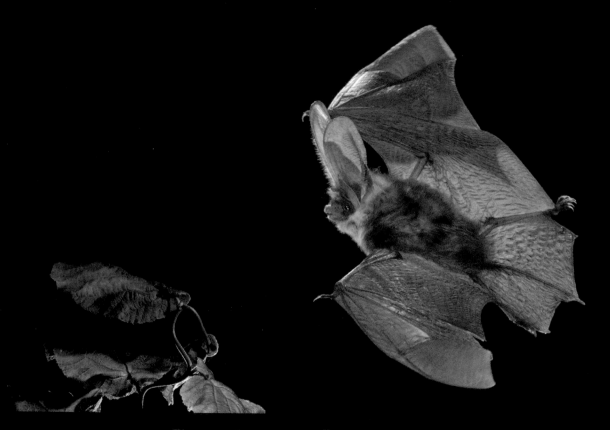

Brown Long-eared Bat *Plecotus auritus*
EURASIA

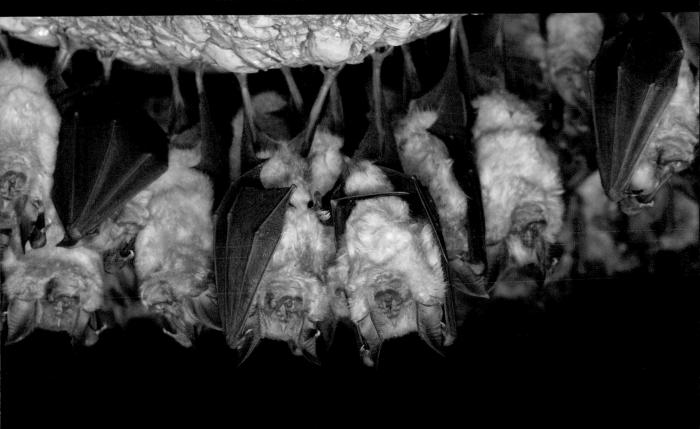

Lesser Mouse-eared Bat *Myotis blythii*

Ground Pangolin *Smutsia temminckii*

SUB-SAHARAN AFRICA

Cheetah *Acinonyx jubatus*

AFRICA AND SOUTH-WEST ASIA

Ocelot *Leopardus pardalis*
SOUTH AMERICA AND CENTRAL AMERICA

Oncilla *Leopardus tigrinus*
SOUTH AMERICA AND CENTRAL AMERICA

Eurasian Lynx *Lynx lynx*
EURASIA

Clouded Leopard *Neofelis nebulosa*
SOUTH ASIA

Lion *Panthera leo*
AFRICA AND SOUTH-WEST ASIA

Jaguar *Panthera onca*
SOUTH AMERICA AND CENTRAL AMERICA

Leopard *Panthera pardus*
AFRICA AND ASIA

Tiger *Panthera tigris*
ASIA

Snow Leopard *Uncia uncia*
ASIA

Masked Palm Civet *Paguma larvata*

ASIA

Cape Genet *Genetta tigrina*
SOUTHERN AFRICA

Fossa *Cryptoprocta ferox*
MADAGASCAR

Banded Mongoose *Mungos mungo*
SUB-SAHARAN AFRICA

Meerkat *Suricata suricatta*
SOUTHERN AFRICA

Spotted Hyena *Crocuta crocuta*
SUB-SAHARAN AFRICA

Aardwolf *Proteles cristata*
AFRICA

Wolf *Canis lupus*

NORTHERN HEMISPHERE

Black-backed Jackal *Canis mesomelas*
SUB-SAHARAN AFRICA

Maned Wolf *Chrysocyon brachyurus*
SOUTH AMERICA

African Wild Dog *Lycaon pictus*
SUB-SAHARAN AFRICA

Bat-eared Fox *Otocyon megalotis*
SUB-SAHARAN AFRICA

Arctic Fox *Vulpes lagopus*
ARCTIC CIRCUMPOLAR

Red Fox　*Vulpes vulpes*

NORTHERN HEMISPHERE

Giant Panda *Ailuropoda melanoleuca*
CHINA

American Black Bear   *Ursus americanus*
NORTH AMERICA

Polar Bear *Ursus maritimus*
ARCTIC CIRCUMPOLAR

Cape Fur Seal *Arctocephalus pusillus pusillus*
SOUTHERN AFRICA

New Zealand Sea-lion *Phocarctos hookeri*

NEW ZEALAND

Walrus *Odobenus rosmarus*
ARCTIC CIRCUMPOLAR

Leopard Seal *Hydrurga leptonyx*
ANTARCTIC CIRCUMPOLAR

Southern Elephant Seal *Mirounga leonina*
ANTARCTIC CIRCUMPOLAR

Harp Seal *Pagophilus groenlandicus*
ARCTIC CIRCUMPOLAR

Oriental Small-clawed Otter *Aonyx cinerea*
SOUTH-EAST ASIA

Sea Otter *Enhydra lutris*
NORTH PACIFIC OCEAN

Giant Otter *Pteronura brasiliensis*
SOUTH AMERICA

Hog Badger *Arctonyx collaris*
SOUTH-EAST ASIA

Wolverine *Gulo gulo*

NORTH OF NORTHERN HEMISPHERE

Pine Marten *Martes martes*

EUROPE

European Badger *Meles meles*
EURASIA

Honey Badger *Mellivora capensis*
AFRICA, MIDDLE EAST AND SOUTH ASIA

Steppe Polecat *Mustela eversmanii*
EURASIA

European Mink *Mustela lutreola*

EUROPE

Weasel *Mustela nivalis*

EURASIA AND NORTH AMERICA

Eastern Spotted Skunk *Spilogale putorius*
NORTH AMERICA

South American Coati *Nasua nasua*
SOUTH AMERICA

Kinkajou *Potos flavus*
CENTRAL AMERICA AND SOUTH AMERICA

North American Raccoon *Procyon lotor*
NORTH AMERICA

Red Panda *Ailurus fulgens*

ASIA

Burchell's Zebra *Equus burchellii*

SUB-SAHARAN AFRICA

Kiang *Equus kiang*
ASIA

South American Tapir *Tapirus terrestris*
SOUTH AMERICA

Black Rhinoceros *Diceros bicornis*
SUB-SAHARAN AFRICA

Common Warthog *Phacochoerus africanus*
SUB-SAHARAN AFRICA

Wild Boar *Sus scrofa*
EURASIA AND NORTH AFRICA

Collared Peccary   *Pecari tajuca*
THE AMERICAS

White-lipped Peccary *Tayassu pecari*
CENTRAL AMERICA AND SOUTH AMERICA

Pygmy Hippopotamus *Hexaprotodon liberiensis*
WEST AFRICA

Common Hippopotamus *Hippopotamus amphibius*

Bactrian Camel *Camel bactrianus*

ASIA

Guanaco *Lama glama*

SOUTH AMERICA

Vicuña *Vicugna vicugna*
SOUTH AMERICA

Lesser Mouse-deer *Tragulus kanchil*
SOUTH-EAST ASIA

Siberian Musk Deer *Moschus moschiferus*

EAST ASIA

Moose *Alces alces*

NORTH AMERICA

Roe Deer *Capreolus capreolus*
EURASIA

Reindeer or Caribou *Rangifer tarandus*
ARCTIC CIRCUMPOLAR

Fallow Deer *Dama dama*
ASIA, INTRODUCED WORLDWIDE

Pronghorn *Antilocapra americana*
NORTH AMERICA

Giraffe *Giraffa camelopardalis*
AFRICA

Okapi *Okapia johnstoni*
WEST AFRICA

Impala *Aepyceros melampus*
EASTERN AND SOUTHERN AFRICA

Blue Wildebeest *Connochaetes taurinus*
EASTERN AND SOUTHERN AFRICA

Springbok *Antidorcas marsupialis*
SOUTHERN AFRICA

Kirk's Dikdik *Madoqua kirkii*
EASTERN AFRICA

Steppe Saiga *Saiga tatarica*
ASIA

American Bison *Bison bison*
NORTH AMERICA

Gaur *Bos frontalis*
SOUTH ASIA

African Buffalo *Syncerus caffer*
SOUTHERN AFRICA

Greater Kudu *Tragelaphus strepsiceros*
SOUTHERN AFRICA

Siberian Ibex *Capra sibirica*

ASIA

Bighorn Sheep *Ovis canadensis*
NORTH AMERICA

Alpine Chamois *Rupicapra rupicapra*
EUROPE

Gemsbok *Oryx gazella*
SOUTHERN AFRICA

Waterbuck *Kobus ellipsiprymnus*
SOUTHERN AFRICA

Blue Whale   *Balaenoptera musculus*
OCEANS WORLDWIDE

Humpback Whale   *Megaptera novaeangliae*
OCEANS WORLDWIDE

Orca   *Orcinus orca*
OCEANS WORLDWIDE

Bottlenose Dolphin *Tursiops truncatus*
OCEANS WORLDWIDE

Narwhal *Monodon monoceros*
ARCTIC OCEANS

Harbour Porpoise *Phocoena phocoena*
NORTH ATLANTIC, NORTH PACIFIC AND BLACK SEA

Sperm Whale *Physeter catodon*
OCEANS WORLDWIDE

Ganges River Dolphin *Platanista gangetica*
INDIAN SUBCONTINENT

Amazon River Dolphin *Inia geoffrensis*
SOUTH AMERICA

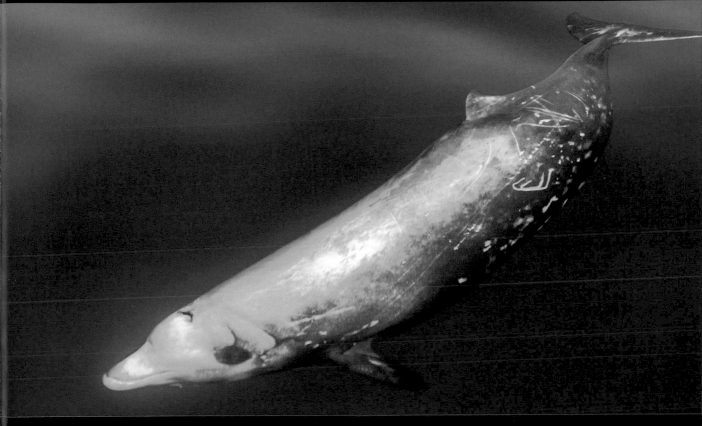

Cuvier's Beaked Whale *Ziphius cavirostris*
OCEANS WORLDWIDE

A Tribute to the Reptiles and Amphibians of Australia and New Zealand
Australian Herpetological Society
ISBN 978 1 92554 659 0

Australian Wildlife On Your Doorstep
Stephanie Jackson
ISBN 978 1 92554 630 9

Crocodiles of the World
Colin Stevenson
ISBN 978 1 92554 628 6

Insects of the World
Paul Zborowski
ISBN 978 1 92554 609 5

Rainforests of Australia's East Coast
Peter Krisch
ISBN 978 1 92554 629 3

Tropical Marine Life of Australia
Graham Edgar
ISBN 978 1 92151 758 7

Wild Dives
Nick and Caroline Robertson-Brown
ISBN 978 1 92554 642 2

Wild Leadership
Erna Walraven
ISBN 978 1 92554 635 4

In the same series as this title:
World of Birds
ISBN 978 1 92554 652 1

World of Reptiles
ISBN 978 1 92554 653 8

World of Insects
ISBN 978 1 92554 651 4

For details of these books and hundreds of other Natural History titles see
www.newhollandpublishers.com
and follow ReedNewHolland
on Facebook and Instagram

First published in 2020 by Reed New Holland Publishers
Sydney • Auckland

Level 1, 178 Fox Valley Road, Wahroonga, NSW 2076, Australia
5/39 Woodside Avenue, Northcote, Auckland 0627, New Zealand

www.newhollandpublishers.com

A record of this book is held at the National Library of Australia.

ISBN 978 1 92554 660 6

Group Managing Director: Fiona Schultz
Publisher and Project Editor: Simon Papps
Designer: Andrew Davies
Production Director: Arlene Gippert
Printer: Toppan Leefung Printing Limited

10 9 8 7 6 5 4 3 2 1

Keep up with Reed New Holland
and New Holland Publishers
 ReedNewHolland
 @NewHollandPublishers and @ReedNewHolland

Front cover: Leopard *Panthera pardus* (Felidae).
Back cover: Red Kangaroo *Macropus rufus* (Macropodidae).
Page 1: Dog (Canidae).
Pages 2–3: Fox (Canidae).
Page 6: Indian Rhinoceros *Rhinoceros unicornis* (Rhinocerotidae).